MYRTL

The Delaplaine
2022 Long Weekend Guide

Andrew Delaplaine

Senior Writer - **James Cubby**

MYRTLE BEACH
The Delaplaine
Long Weekend Guide

TABLES OF CONTENTS

Chapter 1
WHY MYRTLE BEACH?

Yes, I've traveled the world from New York to London, Paris and Rome and lot of little country towns in between, but I spent my teenage years in this little seaside town in what even then was called (rather optimistically, we thought at the time), "The Grand Strand."

We moved into a grand two-story house right across from the beach. We lived on the upper floor and rented out the lower floor to tourists during the summer season for extra income. I can still remember my mother going out to hang the "Vacancy" sign on a swinging shingle. It read, simply and accurately enough, "The Beach House."

Well, those days are LONG gone, buster. The town typified by hundreds of modest beachside cottages has given way to tall high-rise hotels and condos. It looks more like the Florida towns of Hallandale or Sunny Isles than the Myrtle Beach I remember.

The arcades I remember as a kid are still there, though of course very much more high-tech than they used to be. That feeling of being at a carnival or a county fair, a sense of the Midway—that feeling is still a part of Myrtle Beach's little downtown. I don't think that will ever go away.

Or that tension in the air that convinces you (correctly) that every teenager coming here in the summer is looking to get laid. That won't go away either. (It'll happen here more likely than it will at home.)

The big Ferris Wheel is really something. And the big music shows you get at Legends and other places tell you the Big Money has arrived. And it's here to stay.

Myrtle Beach has got to the ultimate location for the family-friendly vacation. There are dozens of great activities for kids.

MURRELLS INLET
Though it's only a few miles south of Myrtle Beach, Murrells Inlet can take an hour to get to at the height of the season. Still worth the trip. There are a couple of really great restaurants down here (as well as a few dive bars). Try to make time to visit **Atalaya Castle**, an old and unusual home built in the 1930s by

Archer and Anna Huntington. Archer donated the land where the nearby **Brookgreen Gardens** was created. Brookgreen is also a must-see place. (Ann's sculpture is on prominent display at Brookgreen.)

Famed pulp crime writer **Mickey Spillane** (1918-2006) lived in Murrells Inlet. (He created the character Mike Hammer.) Legend has it that he saw Murrells Inlet when flying over it in a plane and said, "That's where I want to live." And he did move down, living here for the rest of his life.

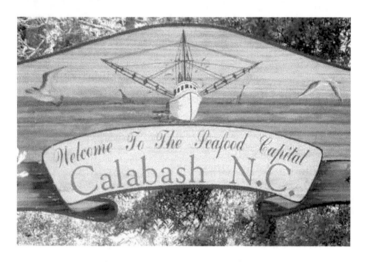

CALABASH

North of Myrtle Beach you'll find the small town of Calabash. They catch most of the seafood you eat right out of the inlet here. One seafood shack after another and they'll all pretty good.

PAWLEYS ISLAND is just a few miles south. This is where you'll go to buy an **Original Pawleys Island Rope Hammock** (assuming that you want one). Since there's no parking to speak of, the beaches aren't as crowded as they might otherwise be (which is why it's such a great place to go, especially on a weekday).

There are a couple of little places, **Sea View Inn** and the **Pelican Inn**, where you can stay if you want to keep the mayhem up in Myrtle Beach at arm's length.

Chapter 2
WHERE TO STAY

Note that when the term "efficiency" is used, it means there's a small kitchen in the room.

THE BREAKERS RESORT
2006 SE Ocean Blvd at 21st and 27th Ave, 855-861-9550
www.breakers.com
There used to be an old hotel on this site made of wood, with large porches that caught the ocean breezes before air conditioning. (I worked there as a night clerk in high school in the 1960s.) It's been replaced by a modern building with good rates. Very

family-friendly. (They actually have 2 locations, here at 21st Ave and up at 27th.)

CROWN REEF RESORT
2913 S Ocean Blvd, 800-291-6598
www.crownreef.com
Crown Reef Resort in Myrtle Beach features over 500 oceanfront rooms and suites with private balconies. Crown Reef amenities and services include: over 20 pools, spas, and fountains, two restaurants, an oceanfront lounge, on-site golf department, game room, oceanfront fitness center, free internet and airport shuttle.

DUNES VILLAGE RESORT
5200 N Ocean Blvd, 855-340-7301
www.dunesvillage.com
In its combined two phases, has the most substantial indoor water park complex ever built at a comparable oceanfront resort in the Myrtle Beach area. The combined water parks consist of a 30,000 square foot

facility featuring an array of water attractions designed to wow guests, including a 250+-ft long river ride, Myrtle Beach's first adult sized indoor waterslides, a massive swimming pool with water volleyball and basketball, a variety of hot tubs, kiddies wet deck with Silly Submarine and a kiddies play pool offering a delightful selection of games and slides. Studios, 1, 2, 3, and 4 bedroom condos.

HAMPTON INN & SUITES OCEANFRONT RESORT
1801 S Ocean Blvd, 877-946-6400
www.hamptoninnoceanfront.com
You've never stayed in a Hampton Inn like this. It's got two larger towers and 7 pools (9 if you want to count the Jacuzzi and the Lazy River). There's a massive crowd for breakfast in the 2 rooms dedicated to serving the hoards.

LONG BAY RESORT
7200 N Ocean Blvd, 855-820-4751
www.longbayresort.com
A family oriented property with numerous pools, sauna, exercise equipment and game room. Two choices for dining as well as Starbucks on site. Conveniently located to several shopping options, lots of dining choices, award winning shows and several golf courses. A wide variety of lodging options: oceanfront rooms, suites and 3 bedroom condos. All units are equipped with free hi-speed wireless Internet access.

MARRIOTT RESORT & SPA AT GRANDE DUNES

8400 Costa Verde Dr, 843-449-8880
www.marriott.com
Very grand hotel and Spa right on the water.

MYRTLE BEACH RESORT

5905 S Kings Highway, 888-826-4018
www.myrtle-beach-resort.com
The Myrtle Beach Resort is a 33-acre, gated complex just south of the city limit. Lodgings include efficiencies (with kitchens), studios and 1, 2 or 3 bedrooms. Available views include direct oceanfront, ocean view (side of ocean front building) and park view. Also a water park with lazy river, an oceanfront cabana bar, 6 pools (1 beach front, 2 indoors), lighted tennis courts, saunas, Jacuzzis and exercise rooms.

OCEAN REEF RESORT

7100 N Ocean Blvd, 855-571-0904
www.oceanreefmyrtlebeach.com
Oceanfront rooms and efficiencies (with kitchens)
and "angle oceanfront" condos with 1, 2, 3 or 4
bedrooms. Family-orientated resort also offers a
children's waterpark, lazy river, Cafe Du Port. All
rooms are equipped with hi-speed wireless Internet
access.

PELICAN INN

506 Myrtle Ave, Pawleys Island, 843-325-7522
www.pawleyspelican.com
This B&B on Pawleys Island (to the south of Myrtle
Beach), like the **Sea View Inn** listed below, is right
on the water and is backed up by a salt marsh where
you can go crabbing. This house was built in the
1840s (but don't freak out, it's fully air conditioned).
Because the Pelican is behind the highest dunes on
the island, it's weathered hurricanes better than other
houses situated here. Memorial Day through Labor
Day. (Breakfast and a mid-day meal are served.)

SEA VIEW INN

414 Myrtle Ave, Pawleys Island, 843-237-4253
www.seaviewinn.net
Hard to beat this getaway spot on Pawleys Island.
This house is right on the ocean. Out back is a salt
marsh. Relax and go crabbing. The inn was built in
1937. (There's a cottage out back with a few rooms as
well.) Rustic, refreshingly unspoiled. Rice planters
used to come to Pawleys Island in the 18th and 19th
centuries to escape the heat on the mainland. Now

you can see what attracted them. (They serve 3 meals a day to guests, starting with morning coffee at 7, followed by breakfast at 8:30. Mid-day meal is served at 1:15 and an evening meal at 6:30. Good Southern cooking.)

SHERATON MYRTLE BEACH CONVENTION CENTER HOTEL
2101 N Oak Ave, 843-918-5000
www.sheratonmyrtlebeach.com
All the amenities you expect from a Sheraton inn.

Chapter 3
WHERE TO EAT

ABUELO'S
Coastal Grand Mall
740 Coastal Grand Cir, Myrtle Beach, 843-448-5533
www.abuelos.com
CUISINE: Mexican/Tex-Mex
DRINKS: Full bar
SERVING: Lunch & Dinner
PRICE RANGE: $$

Texas-based chain family restaurant offering authentic Mexican fare (more Tex-Mex, really) in a big open room with an eye-pleasing arched colonnade punctuated with plants. There are some booths against the wall on the other side of the arches if you want a little privacy. Spacious bar is nice. Favorites: Steak & Shrimp Fajitas; Enchiladas; and Medallion chicken. Happy hour with food specials. Kids menu. Some outdoor seating, but it overlooks a spiritless parking lot.

ASPEN GRILL
5101 N Kings Hwy, Myrtle Beach, 843-449-9191
www.aspen-grille.com
CUISINE: American (New)
DRINKS: Full bar

SERVING: Dinner; closed Monday
PRICE RANGE: $$$
Upscale eatery offering a menu of traditional American and Southern cuisine. Menu picks: Filet Mignon and Pan Seared Flounder & Shrimp. Great cocktails. Live jazz nights.

ATLAS TAP HOUSE
1004 Chester St, Myrtle Beach, 843-945-9122
www.atlastaphouse.com
CUISINE: BBQ
DRINKS: Full bar
SERVING: Dinner, Lunch on Sat & Sun
PRICE RANGE: $$
Popular hangout offering an impressive selection of craft beers. Simple menu of burgers and BBQ sandwiches. Choice spot for their Sunday Recovery Brunch serving bottomless Mimosas. Locals spend time here playing an assortment of board games and darts.

BIG MIKE'S SOUL FOOD
504 16th Ave N, Myrtle Beach, 843-712-2048
www.bigmikessoulfood.net
CUISINE: Soul Food
DRINKS: No Booze
SERVING: Lunch/Dinner; closed Sunday
PRICE RANGE: $
NEIGHBORHOOD: East End
Comfortable eatery offering up large servings of Southern comfort food. Menu picks: Fried chicken and Big Mike's Burger & fries.

BONEFISH GRILL
7401 N Kings Hwy, Myrtle Beach, 843-497-5294
www.bonefishgrill.com
CUISINE: Seafood
DRINKS: Full bar
SERVING: Dinner, Lunch on Sat & Sun
PRICE RANGE: $$
NEIGHBORHOOD: East End
Bright contemporary grill with a simple menu of
seafood and steaks. Menu picks: Bang Bang Tacos
and Atlantic salmon. Very casual.

CAPTAIN GEORGE'S SEAFOOD RESTAURANT

1401 29th Ave N, Myrtle Beach, 843-916-2278

https://captaingeorges.com

CUISINE: Seafood
DRINKS: Full bar
SERVING: Dinner; Lunch & Dinner on Sundays
PRICE RANGE: $$$

Relaxed, nautical-themed eatery with a vast seafood buffet that draws a crowd with an all-you-can-eat option for those with big appetites. It's in a big modern building. Inside, someone had the bright idea of fashioning some masts and yardarms over the huge salad bar, with sails drooping down and the rigging all over the place. The variety of seafood is endless—king crab legs, blue claw crabs, mussels, clams, oysters, salmon, oysters, but they also serve steaks, salads, and desserts. Thankfully, there's a bar, so it's possible to escape the madness of the dining room. There's also an *a la carte* menu if you want to avoid the crush of the hunger-crazed hoard descending on the buffet.

CAROLINA ROADHOUSE

4617 N Kings Hwy, Myrtle Beach, 843-497-9911
www.carolinaroadhouse.com
CUISINE: Steakhouse/American (Traditional)
DRINKS: Full bar
SERVING: Lunch & Dinner
PRICE RANGE: $$

Popular eatery with a bar/lodge atmosphere. It's one of those places that usually has a line and can handle large numbers of tourists. There are lots of booths, so try to get one of those, or escape to the big spacious bar area. The wooden interior is softened by a couple of palm trees. The large menu of American fare including lots of Southern favorites like Baby Back Ribs (these are damned good!) and the Killer Dog (a foot-long hot dog doused with chili, cheese, and thick-cut fries). Long wraparound bar with TVs for sports fans.

CIAO
5223 N Kings Highway, 843-449-5700
www.ciaomyrtlebeach.com
CUISINE: Italian
DRINKS: Beer & wine
SERVING: Lunch & dinner daily (except when closed Sunday)
PRICE RANGE: $$
You'd drive right past this unpretentious place in a stripe mall, but know this: it's widely preferred by locals. It's good to book a table as it fills up quite fast. Baked clams, mussels marinana, spaghetti carbonara, manicotti. All the chicken and veal Italian favorites here in this family-run place.

CROISSANTS BISTRO & BAKERY
3751 Robert M Grissom Pkwy, Myrtle Beach, 843-448-2253
www.croissants.net
CUISINE: Bakery/Seafood/Comfort Food

DRINKS: Full bar
SERVING: 7 a.m. – 6 p.m.
PRICE RANGE: $$
Bakery with a menu of American comfort food and seafood. The bakery has a dozen or so tables off to the side. Lots of pastries, croissants, and cookies. (The choice of locals when they shop for wedding cakes.) Popular breakfast spot for items like the lump crabmeat benedict and the build-your-own-omelet. Also several crepe dishes. (Make sure you get a side of what they call "cheesy hash browns"—they are scrumptious.) There's a full bar, and the day I was there you could make your own bloody Mary and garnish it at the bar.

DAGWOOD'S DELI
400 11th Ave N, Myrtle Beach, 843-448-0100
600 Hwy 17 N, Surfside Beach, 843-828-4600
(Sports Bar)
www.dagwoodsdeli.com
CUISINE: Deli
DRINKS: Full bar
SERVING: 11 a.m. – 4 p.m.; Closed Sundays
PRICE RANGE: $
Sandwich shop specializing in jumbo-size sandwiches made using fresh bread with interesting flavors like Cheddar Bacon (flavors change daily). The sandwiches are overstuffed with an amazing selection of sides. Like the Chicken Fritters or the Jalapeno Poppers. Big selection of Quesadillas. The Surfside location is a sports bar with 3 or 4 dozen TV screens. (It's a lot to deal with!)

DRUNKEN JACK'S RESTAURANT & LOUNGE

4031 Highway 17 Business, Murrells Inlet, 843-651-2044

www.drunkenjacks.com

CUISINE: American
DRINKS: Full Bar
SERVING: Dinner
PRICE RANGE: $$$

A little pricey for what you get, but there's a great view overlooking the Inlet. Shrimp & crab fondue is a nice different dish; she crab soup; Southwestern eggroll; lots of different seafood platter combinations to choose from on this large menu; but also frog legs, soft shell crabs. Full selection of steaks.

FIRE AND SMOKE GASTROPUB

411 79th Ave N, Myrtle Beach, 843-449-0085

https://www.facebook.com/fireandsmoke.agastropub/

CUISINE: Steakhouse
DRINKS: Full bar
SERVING: Dinner
PRICE RANGE: $$$

Gastropub/steakhouse offering upscale American fare. White tablecloths at night. Booths against the wall. Much cozier and swanky than your usual Myrtle Beach options. Nice little bar. Favorites: Crispy Pork with Grits & Collards; Smoked Bison with Wild Boar Meatloaf, Kansas City style bone-in strip steak; and Lobster Tail Tempura. Handcrafted cocktails and eclectic choice of microbrews.

HOOK & BARREL
8014 N Kings Hwy, Myrtle Beach, 843-839-5888
www.hookandbarrelrestaurant.com
CUISINE: Seafood
DRINKS: Full bar
SERVING: Dinner; Brunch on Sunday
PRICE RANGE: $$

A "nautical" eatery offering a menu of local seafood.
A wonderful bar has three long sides and is very
comfortable, with jellyfish-like lighting fixtures
hanging from above that change colors. Popular
Sunday brunch destination. You can have your fresh

fish prepared 4 ways—baked, grilled, pan-seared or blackened. A choice of spicy sauces also comes with the fish. Favorites: Pineapple shrimp fried rice and crab cakes. (Get a side of the parmesan & rosemary fries.) Nice wine selection. Happy hour. Outdoor seating on the long porch is very nice.

LEE'S INLET KITCHEN
4460 Highway 17, Murrells Inlet, 843-651-2881
www.leesinletkitchen.com
CUISINE: Seafood
DRINKS: Full Bar
SERVING: Dinner

PRICE RANGE: $$
You don't want to leave this great place without tasting the she-crab soup. (Get the hushpuppies to go with it.) The place is a little rundown and it looks like they haven't changed anything since they opened in 1940s. (They call it "charm.") Food is generally very good. Focus on the seafood, of course.

LIBRARY
6613 N Kings Hwy, Myrtle Beach, 843-448-4527
www.thelibraryrestaurantsc.com
CUISINE: French/Steakhouse
DRINKS: Full bar
SERVING: Dinner; closed Sunday
PRICE RANGE: $$$$
Excellent upscale dining with select dishes prepared tableside. House favorite: Steak Diane and sweetbreads flamed tableside. Impressive wine list.

LULU'S CAFÉ
1903 N Ocean Blvd, Myrtle Beach, 843-712-1890

No Website
CUISINE: Diner/American (Traditional)
DRINKS: Full bar
SERVING: Breakfast, Lunch & Dinner
PRICE RANGE: $
'50s style diner offering a great all-American menu. Popular for its creative breakfast menu with dishes like Monterey scrambled eggs with spinach and shrimp. Indoor & outdoor seating.

MARGARITAVILLE

114 Celebrity Cir, Broadway at the Beach, Myrtle Beach, 843-448-5455
www.margaritavillemyrtlebeach.com
CUISINE: Bakery/American (Traditional)
DRINKS: Full bar
SERVING: Lunch & Dinner
PRICE RANGE: $$
I don't know if it's Jimmy Buffett's music that made him rich—or crowd-pleasing places like this. Located on a permanently docked boat (the not-quite accurately named *Euphoria*), this unique (that's not necessarily a compliment) eatery serves up standard American fare (emphasis on "standard") and what passes for "tropical" cocktails in non-tropical towns. Menu picks: Chicken quesadillas and Peel & Eat shrimp. And of course, the 'incredible' margaritas. Completely phony "island-themed" restaurant, but it's hard to pinpoint the island they had in mind. All my snarky kidding aside, the food is not bad, not bad at all, as long as you avoid the Volcano Nachos. The Caribbean Chicken Egg Roles are great. What I like most about this place is watching the truckloads of

people surge through the place. As sobering and shuddering as it is, *that* is a sight to see.

MEDIEVAL TIMES
2904 Fantasy Way, 888-935-6878
www.medievaltimes.com
CUISINE: American
DRINKS: Full Bar
SERVING: Dinner
PRICE RANGE: $$$
Medieval Times is the best value for your money. This imaginative new entertainment spot was inspired by the true medieval tradition of royal families inviting guests to a festival and feast to watch knights compete on horseback. Guests are encouraged to be interactive by sitting in colored sections and cheering for their knight. Weapons and costumes are very accurate and the characters and storyline have

evolved. At Medieval Times, you get Dinner and a tournament entertainment.

MR. FISH
6401 N Kings Hwy, Myrtle Beach, (843) 839-3474
www.mrfish.com
CUISINE: Sushi Bar/Seafood/Southern
DRINKS: Full bar
SERVING: Dinner; Closed Sun - Tues
PRICE RANGE: $$
Seafood market and eatery. Fresh seafood daily including filleted fish and soft-shell crabs. Favorites: Fried whole small flounder; Shrimp & Grits; Fried shrimp platter; Fried oysters; excellent tuna sandwich. (You'll get free hush puppies served with a honey butter—don't fill up on them.) The market offers their homemade soups, an excellent selection of spices, homemade sauces and merchandise with the Mr. Fish logo.

NEW YORK PRIME
405 28th Ave N, Myrtle Beach, 843) 448-8081
www.newyorkprime.com
CUISINE: Steakhouse
DRINKS: Full bar
SERVING: Dinner
PRICE RANGE: $$$$

High-end steakhouse in a rather ordinary room (but they do have white tablecloths), but the room is not as important as the food here. The service is impeccable. A welcome respite from the slapdash service one expects at the dozens of common-denominator tourist traps in Myrtle Beach serving almost always the exact same menu items. (Another order of Nachos,

anybody?) Here they offer an impressive menu of
USDA prime-only steaks, lobster, seafood dishes &
classic sides. Favorites: Sea Bass for those of you not
eating a steak. All steaks are aged 28 days at least,
and served Pittsburgh-style, with a charred exterior
and juicy inside. You can't go wrong here. A nice bar
area as well, which is where you'll find me when I
stop in. Very good wine selection.

PAULA DEEN'S FAMILY KITCHEN
1202 Celebrity Cir, Myrtle Beach, 843-945-1072
www.pauladeensfamilykitchen.com
CUISINE: American (Traditional)/Southern
DRINKS: Beer & Wine
SERVING: Breakfast, Lunch, and Dinner
PRICE RANGE: $$
Celebrity-owned eatery serving family-style classic
Southern fare in a huge sprawling building where the
restaurant is forced to share space with a store that
sells "Everything Paula." This is one of those big
places (like Jimmy Buffett's Margaritaville) that must
churn out the cash. It doesn't even have the charm of
a Denny's. Just a big space jammed with people. No
décor to speak of. But who needs it? There's even an
escalator to keep the crowds moving. The portions are
big so come with an appetite because they don't let
you take anything to go. The food? Undeniably good.
I love this stuff. Favorites: Fried chicken; Chicken-
fried pork chop; Fried Okra; and Pepper steak.
Candied yams are mouthwatering. The ooey-gooey
cake is outrageous. That's enough. I'm getting hungry
just thinking about that blazing good pork chop I had
last trip. You go, Paula!

POP POP'S PIT BBQ

8724 Hwy 707, Myrtle Beach, 843-650-9227
www.poppopspitbbq.com
CUISINE: BBQ
DRINKS: Beer & Wine
SERVING: Lunch & Dinner; closed Sunday
PRICE RANGE: $$
Simple menu of BBQ dishes like brisket and pulled pork. Typical sides like baked beans and mac and cheese.

PULASKI DELI

2701 N Kings Hwy, Ste 1, Myrtle Beach, 843-443-6444

www.pulaski-deli.com

CUISINE: Polish/Deli

DRINKS: Full bar

SERVING: Lunch/Dinner, Lunch only on Sunday

PRICE RANGE: $$

NEIGHBORHOOD: East End

Market and Polish restaurant all-in-one. Great sandwiches and traditional dishes like pierogi, cabbage rolls and Polska kielbasa. Shop has souvenirs and gifts.

RIOZ BRAZILIAN STEAKHOUSE

2920 Hollywood Drive, Myrtle Beach, 843-839-0777

1315 Hwy 17 N, North Myrtle Beach, 843-492-9777

www.rioz.com

CUISINE: Brazilian/Steakhouse

DRINKS: Full bar

SERVING: Dinner

PRICE RANGE: $$$

Upscale Brazilian steakhouse (or *churrascaria*, as they would call it) featuring an impressive menu of flame-broiled meats (pork loin, sirloin, beef ribs, pork ribs, beef tenderloin, pork sausage, chicken and leg of lamb). Steaks carved tableside. Don't get drawn in by the HUGE salad bar, probably the biggest you've ever seen. My first trip I filled up on so many items from the salad bar I couldn't eat any meat at dinner. (This happens more than you think.) The good thing is—you can order just the salad bar. Favorites: Filet

mignon wrapped in bacon and Double lamb chops.
Classic cocktails.

RIVER CITY CAFÉ
404 21st Ave N, North Myrtle Beach, 843-448-1990
www.rivercitycafe.com
CUISINE: American (Traditional)
DRINKS: Full bar
SERVING: Lunch/Dinner
PRICE RANGE: $$
Casual eatery with butcher paper on the tables. Don't
come here if you have a peanut allergy as there are
peanuts and shells everywhere. Typical American
menu of giant burgers and wings.

ROCKEFELLERS RAW BAR
3613 Highway 17 S, North Myrtle Beach, 843-361-9677
www.rockefellersrawbar.com
CUISINE: Seafood/American (Traditional)
DRINKS: Full bar
SERVING: Lunch & Dinner
PRICE RANGE: $$
Casual eatery featuring a menu of homemade
American fare. Known for seafood cooked in steam
kettles. Favorites: they'd have to serve Oysters
Rockefeller, of course, and they are really good (I had
2 orders); She Crab soup also excellent; Seafood
Platter; Po Boys (choice of oysters, scallops or
shrimp). Happy hour specials.

RUTH'S CHRIS STEAKHOUSE
8211 Marina Pkwy, Myrtle Beach, 843-839-9500

www.ruthschris.net
CUISINE: Steakhouse/Seafood
DRINKS: Full bar
SERVING: Dinner
PRICE RANGE: $$$
Upscale steakhouse chain offering a menu of top-quality beef. Great steaks, salads and desserts. Try the white chocolate bread pudding with liqueur topping. Perfect martinis and nice wine selection. Daily happy hour.

SEA CAPTAIN'S HOUSE
3002 N Ocean Blvd, 843-448-8082
www.seacaptains.com
CUISINE: Seafood
DRINKS: Full Bar
SERVING: Breakfast-Lunch-Dinner
PRICE RANGE: $$
An institution in Myrtle Beach. Definitely don't miss this seafood place.

SIMPLY SOUTHERN SMOKEHOUSE

1913 Mr Joe White Ave, Myrtle Beach, 843-839-1913

www.simplysouthernsmokehouse.com

CUISINE: Southern/Smokehouse/BBQ
DRINKS: No Booze
SERVING: Lunch & Dinner; Lunch only on Sun & Mon
PRICE RANGE: $$

The name says it all. Simply Southern Smokehouse BBQ and Soul food. Maybe it's the harsh fluorescent lights blaring down too brightly over every table. Or maybe because they don't serve booze. Whatever. Not my favorite place. Here you'll get Southern cooking like your grandmother made (as long as she was from the South and *not* a gourmet). Food served buffet style. Favorites: Grilled pork chops and Pulled BBQ (4 different styles of sauce). Save room for the Peach cobbler. This place attracts the tourist bus crowd, so you've been warned. Go early or late, avoiding peak times. Waiters often burst into song. (So do I, but only after 4 drinks, which lamentably, you can't get here.)

STICKY FINGERS

2461 Coastal Grand Cir, Myrtle Beach, 843-839-7427
www.stickyfingers.com
CUISINE: BBQ
DRINKS: Full bar
SERVING: Lunch/Dinner
PRICE RANGE: $$
Classic BBG dishes pit-smoked and covered in their
signature sauces (also available for sale). Favorites:
BBQ nachos with pork and Pecan Pie. Impressive for
a chain.

VINTAGE TWELVE

9800 Queensway Blvd, Ste 109, Myrtle Beach, 843-
497-7300
www.vintagetwelve.com
CUISINE: American (New)/Seafood
DRINKS: Full bar
SERVING: Dinner
PRICE RANGE: $
Located inside the Embassy Suites, this eatery offers
a nice menu including vegetarian and gluten-free
options. Menu picks: Crab cakes and 4 oz. Sirloin.
For dessert try the warmed chocolate chip cookie
served atop bourbon caramel with ice cream.

Chapter 4
WHERE TO SHOP

COASTAL GRAND MALL
2000 Coastal Grand Circle, 843-839-9110
www.coastalgrand.com
A recently-built massive mall that attracts large crowds year-round.

THE GAY DOLPHIN
916 N Ocean Blvd, 843-448-6550
www.gaydolphin.com
The Gay Dolphin claims to be the "nation's largest gift shop." If you're walking along the main strip in Myrtle Beach, the Gay Dolphin is a must see, if just to gawk at their eclectic collection of gifts, ranging from the typical beach trinkets to statues of ancient Egyptian sarcophagi. In the past, you could access the

roof for a great view of the beach, but the roof is no longer open to the public.

ORIGINAL PAWLEY'S ISLAND ROPE HAMMOCK

10880 Ocean Hwy Pawleys Island, 843-237-9122
www.hammockshop.com

Just south of Myrtle Beach, you'll find this great shop selling hammocks and accessories. Here's the story: Back in the late 1800s, this hammock was created by Capt. Joshua Ward to make it easier to sleep during those muggy Low Country nights. Since he was a merchantman who ferried rice from the plantations in the area to port in Georgetown, he knew what a hammock was because sailors commonly slept in them. But those were canvas hammocks. He invented the rope hammock, perfecting the way it is woven together so the knots are on the ends and not in the "bed" of the hammock, and more important, invented the "spreader bar" through which the ropes pass so the hammock doesn't lose its shape. His family's been selling "Cap'n Josh's" hammocks since they opened this store in 1935. And, take it from me, having dozed on in them for many years, they're still the best.

Chapter 5
WHAT TO SEE

BAREFOOT LANDING
4898 Highway 17 S, 843-272-8349
www.bflanding.com
Located along the Intracoastal Waterway at the
intersection of 48th Avenue South and Route 17, it is
the first major tourist center in the area with over 100
shops, great eateries, steakhouses and a brewery,
home to the **Alabama Theatre** and **House of Blues**,
both offering live entertainment nightly.
Entertainment includes live shows, big name
entertainment and great attractions including one of
the largest reptile parks in the world. Kid favorites are

the carousel and fish feeding along with weekly fireworks. Visitors and groups are greeted upon arrival and receive a shopping bag that includes a Preferred Member discount card and list of participating merchants and a free meal voucher.

BROADWAY AT THE BEACH
1325 Celebrity Circle, 843-444-3200
www.broadwayatthebeach.com
A huge cluster of bars, nightlife, shops, a movie theatre and even an aquarium spread out over 700,000 square feet, Broadway stands to be one of Myrtle Beach's more accessible attractions. It is the largest festival entertainment complex in South Carolina featuring theaters, 20 restaurants, over 100 specialty shops, 15 attractions, 11 night clubs, and 3 hotels. It's also crowded, although the Butterfly Pavilion is worth the admission. New additions in 2010 include restaurants and shops for sports, technology, and apparel. Some stores include Ron Jon Surf Shop, Sharkey's Bar & Grill, and XCell Wireless

Technology and Accessories. There is a zip line ride that spans 500 feet back and forth across the 23-acre Lake Broadway.

BROOKGREEN GARDENS
1931 Brookgreen Dr, Murrells Inlet, 843-235-6000
www.brookgreen.org
Lovely gardens, perfectly enchanting, built in the 1930s as a place to showcase, in a natural outdoor setting, some of America's finest sculpture. Prominently displayed are works by sculptors such as Anna Hyatt Huntington. It is the country's first public sculpture garden (opened in 1932) and has the largest collection of figurative sculpture by American artists in an outdoor setting in the world. Over 1,400 sculptures are displayed here. The place takes its name from Brookgreen Plantation, owned by America's largest slaveholder, Joshua John Ward. (In 1850, he owned over 1,000 slaves and was dubbed "king of the rice planters.")

THE CAROLINA OPRY
CALVIN GILMORE THEATER
8901 N Kings Hwy, 800-843-6779
www.thecarolinaopry.com

The Carolina Opry has thrilled the hundreds of thousands of visitors over the years. The award-winning show blends two hours of high-energy music, comedy and dance. The Carolina Opry is the only show to win every major South Carolina tourism award and the only show to be voted the #1 show for over 20 years straight. Other shows include Good Vibrations (music from the '60s, '70s, and '80s), LIGHT - Laser Extravaganza (a music & laser show), and the Carolina Opry Christmas Special.

FAMILY KINGDOM AMUSEMENT PARK
300 S Ocean Blvd, 843-626-3447
www.familykingdomfun.com
This is one of the declining numbers of sea-fronting amusement parks, replete with roller coasters, carousels, cotton candy, the largest Ferris wheel in South Carolina, and a beachfront water park that includes at least six water slides, lots of splashing fountains, and an interconnected series of lazy river-style swimming pools. A few of the park's attractions were salvaged from the Pavilion, a now-defunct venue that evokes nostalgia in the hearts of many local residents. The majority of the park's 30 rides, however, are high-tech enough to generate excitement, and traditional enough to still evoke memories of Clarence the Clown and spun-sugar candy.

MARRIOTT'S OCEAN WATCH AT GRANDE DUNES
8500 Costa Verda Dr, 843-692-5500
www.marriott.com

MYRTLE BEACH FC

This is a pro soccer team playing in the National Premier Soccer League. The team plays at the Doug Shaw Memorial Stadium, located on 33rd Avenue. The regular season runs from May to July and tickets are free for kids aged 10 and under.

MYRTLE BEACH PELICANS

1251 21st Ave N, 843-918-6000
http://www.milb.com/index.jsp?sid=t521
The Pelicans are an Advanced-A Affiliate of the Texas Rangers. The Pelicans' stadium, BB&T Coastal Field, is located at the intersection of 21st Avenue North & Robert Grissom Parkway, directly across from Broadway at the Beach. There have been a few Major League Baseball players who have worn the Pelicans' uniform since the team began play in 1999, such as Rafael Furcal, Marcus Giles, Ryan Langerhans, Horacio Ramirez, Pete Orr, Adam LaRoche, Jeff Francoeur, and Brain McCann.

MYRTLE BEACH SPEEDWAY
455 Hospitality Lane, 843-236-0500
(Located off of Highway 501 entering Myrtle Beach)
www.myrtlebeachspeedway.com
Hosts events weekly such as NASCAR Late Model
Stock Car races, Spring Fling Swap Meet & Car
Shows, the year ending Seneca 400 weekend, and
drifting events. It is a NASCAR Sanctioned .538 mile
short track. For many years, it has been the training
grounds for some of NASCAR's biggest competitors.
Nowhere else can you watch live racing action every
Saturday night on the Grand Strand.

MYRTLE BEACH STATE PARK
4401 S Kings Highway, 843-238-5325
www.myrtlebeachstatepark.net
One of the few underdeveloped natural areas to be
found along the Grand Strand. The 312 acre park
boasts a mile of beachfront and includes a large

campground, a fishing pier and nature trails that lead through a maritime forest. There is a nature center that offers the visitors the chance to learn about dolphins, sea turtles, and the abundant bird and plant life. There is Wi-Fi availability for park guests at the campground store and pier, pets are allowed in most outdoor areas year round, and there are tours and programs for visitors that are fun, engaging, and educational to raise awareness about the natural resources of the park. Myrtle Beach State Park is a "Discover Carolina Site," which provides curriculum-based science programs for school children. Modest admission fee.

MYRTLE WAVES WATER PARK
3000 Mr. Joe White Ave, 843-913-9250
www.myrtlewaves.com
Myrtle Beach is *hot* in summer, so it's little wonder that June through August this park is jampacked with families escaping the heat. The state's largest water park has 1 million gallons and some 20 acres of curves, waves, and swerves. Some 200,000 visitors come annually for the more than 30 rides and various attractions, including an Ocean in Motion Wave pool; the LayZee River, a slow, 3-mph ride around the park; and Bubble Bay, a 7,000-foot leisure pool with a trio of cascading water umbrellas. Other amusements include a Saturation Station with splashes, slides, and waterfalls, including a Caribbean-themed "volcano" -- the world's tallest tubular slides (10 stories high).

PIRATES VOYAGE

8907 N. Kings Hwy, 843-497-9700

www.Piratesvoyage.com

For GPS directions: 8901-B N Kings Hwy.

This is a splashy show you get to watch while you eat a "feast." The Crimson and Sapphire pirates battle each other on deck, in the water and in the sky above their full-sized pirate ships in a 15-foot deep indoor hideaway lagoon. Spectacular acrobatic competition, live animals and a brand new original music score by Dolly Parton creates an immersive experience.

RIPLEY'S AQUARIUM

1110 Celebrity Circle. 800-734-8888 or 843-916-0888

www.ripleys.com

Large aquarium including Touch-a-Ray Bay, Stingray Bay and Sharks.

Chapter 6
GOLF

Although at first glance, one might wonder what made the Grand Strand the "Golf Capital of the World." When I was a teenager living there in the 1960s, there were only a handful of courses, the **Dunes** being the standout at the time, along with **Pine Lakes International Country Club**. Especially at Pine Lakes, you felt like you'd gone back in time. The beautiful green lawn coming down from the clubhouse with its stately white columns, set amid dogwoods, azaleas and magnolias—it was (and is) a picture of the Old South you'll not soon forget. (It was built in 1927 by Henry Bacon McCoy, a project he took on after completing the Lincoln Memorial in Washington.) The majestic clubhouse has over 60 rooms.

The 18 holes comprising the current course were created from the 27 holes designed by creator Robert White, also distinguished because he was the first president of the PGA. He was from St. Andrews, and to this day all the starters and attendants wear the MacGregor tartan.

Back then, we knew that Myrtle Beach was really "in the middle of Nowhere." Yes, it got crowded in the summer, but when I was a bellboy at the Surfwood (a modest 2-story motel on the oceanfront at 29th Avenue), it was still a little Podunk town and we all knew it. (We *liked* it that way and loved the autumn when the tourists left so we could reclaim the town for ourselves.)

A few years later, by the time I had risen to the exalted position of night clerk at The Breakers (yes, we vainly capitalized the "The" the same way they do The Breakers in Palm Beach, though God knows that was the only thing those two properties had in common), golf had gone from golf with a little "g" to Golf with a capital "G."

Suddenly, it seemed like there was a new golf course opening every week.

Now, of course, the area is noted around the world for the dozens and dozens of golf courses sprinkled up and down the coast.

I could write a whole book just on Golf, but I'm not. I'll just refer you to a couple of sites that can get you started if you're new to the area.

MINIATURE GOLF

It wasn't enough for Myrtle Beach to become the Golf Capital of the World. It's also become a **Putt-Putt Capital of the World**, with some of the most innovative and challenging courses in this uniquely American institution.

Remember that lots of these outfits reduce their hours or close altogether off-season.

MT. ATLANTICUS MINI GOLF

http://myrtlebeachminigolf.com/
This sprawling place has two 18-hole mini golf courses.

LIST OF GOLF COURSES
Go to this site for complete information:
www.myrtlebeachgolf.com

MYRTLE BEACH GOLF HOLIDAY
1705 N Oak St #6, Myrtle Beach, 843-477-8833
www.golfholiday.com
Government funded, non-profit organization designed
to provide information on golf in Myrtle Beach. Read
news, find area information, and book over 70
courses and hotels online.

Chapter 7
NIGHTLIFE

THE CAROLINA OPRY
 8901 N Kings Hwy, 800-843-6779 or 843-913-4000
www.thecarolinaopry.com
The Carolina Opry has thrilled the hundreds of
thousands of visitors over the years. The award-

winning show blends two hours of high-energy music, comedy and dance. The Carolina Opry is the only show to win every major South Carolina tourism award and the only show to be voted the #1 show for over 20 years straight. Other shows include Good Vibrations (music from the '60s, '70s, and '80s), LIGHT - Laser Extravaganza (a music & laser show), and the Carolina Opry Christmas Special.

KARMA ULTIMATE TEEN NIGHLIFE
1101 N Ocean Blvd, 843-455-6061
www.karmamb.com **WEBSITE DOWN**
Karma Ultimate Teen Nightlife is exactly as it sounds. They work hard to give teens the best nightlife experience available in a fun yet safe way. Karma was founded in 2006 in by Larry Frakes and Jeff Martin. DJ Jeff Martin was a national touring DJ that has worked for MTV, was resident DJ at the House Of Blues, plus worked in clubs and concert halls across the country. Martin also served as Resident DJ and Talent Coordinator for the legendary Attic Teen Club located at the historic Myrtle Beach Pavilion. After almost 50 years the Attic was torn down in 2005. Martin teamed up with Frakes to create

a place where teen nightlife was brought to a whole new level and Karma was born.

HOUSE OF BLUES
4640 Highway 17 S, North Myrtle Beach, 843-272-3000
www.houseofblues.com

LEGENDS IN CONCERT
2925 Hollywood Dr, 800-960-7469 or 843-238-7827
www.legendsinconcert.com
The World's Greatest Live Tribute Show featuring tributes to stars of today and yesterday such as Elvis Presley, Madonna, Rod Stewart, Michael Jackson, The Temptations, Britney Spears, and more. Legends In Concert's Myrtle Beach production is located at Broadway at the Beach next to Planet Hollywood. Legends opened a brand-new state-of-the-theater in March 2011 in Myrtle Beach. The show features a live band and dancers that accompany all of the legendary stars.

PIRATES VOYAGE
8907 N. Kings Hwy, 843-497-9700
www.Piratesvoyage.com
For GPS directions: 8901-B N Kings Hwy.
This is a splashy show you get to watch while you eat a "feast." The Crimson and Sapphire pirates battle each other on deck, in the water and in the sky above their full-sized pirate ships in a 15-foot deep indoor hideaway lagoon. Spectacular acrobatic competition, live animals and a brand new original music score by Dolly Parton creates an immersive experience.

INDEX

Barbara Krause